MR. OKRA

SELLS FRESH FRUITS AND VEGETABLES

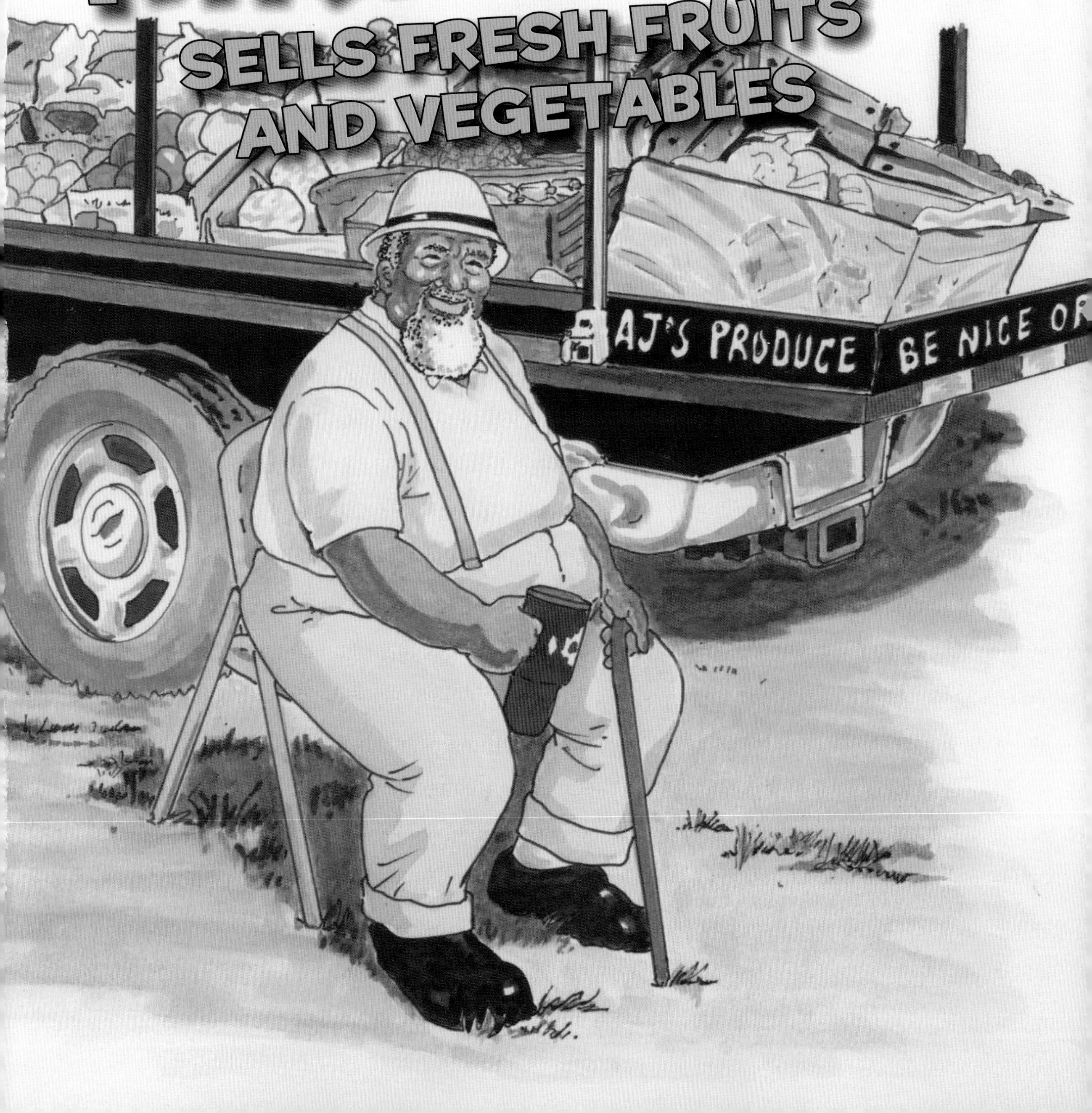

MR. OKRA
SELLS FRESH FRUITS AND VEGETABLES

LASHON DALEY • ILLUSTRATED BY EMILE HENRIQUEZ

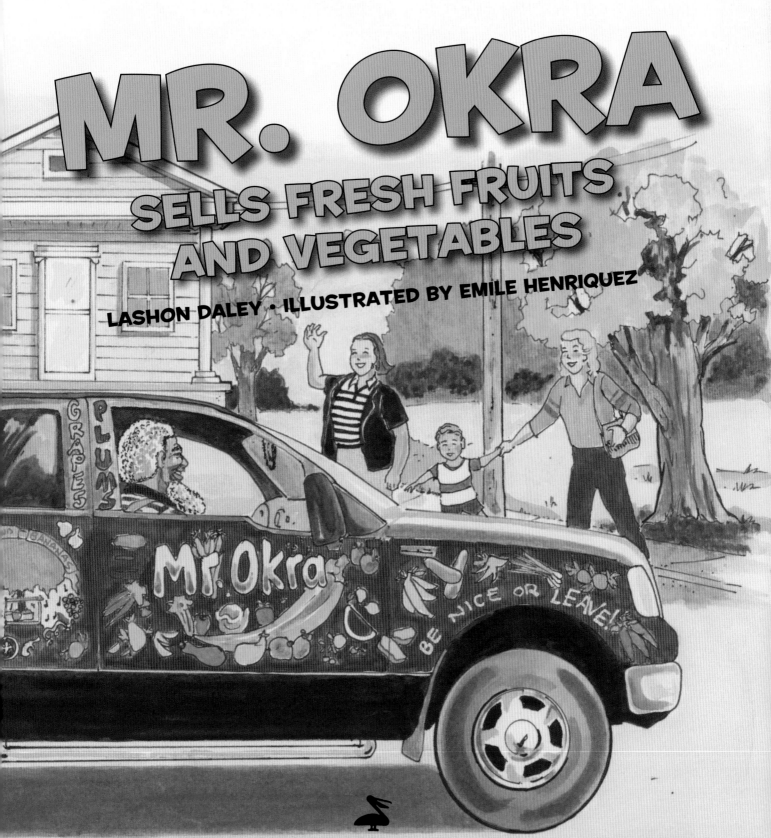

PELICAN PUBLISHING COMPANY
GRETNA 2015

In loving memory of my mother, Audrey

The word "Pelican" and the depiction of a pelican are trademarks of Pelican Publishing Company, Inc., and are registered in the U.S. Patent and Trademark Office.

ISBN: 9781455621125
E-book ISBN: 9781455621132

Printed in Malaysia
Published by Pelican Publishing Company, Inc.
1000 Burmaster Street, Gretna, Louisiana 70053

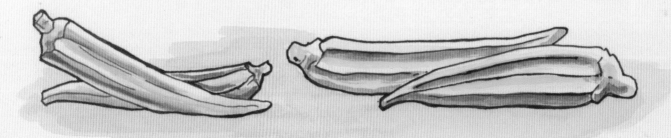

In the morning when the sun rises, Mr. Okra drives his bright **RED** truck through the streets of New Orleans selling fresh fruits and vegetables.

"I got **ORANGES** and **BANANAS**," Mr. Okra sings.

His voice is deep and strong like the musical notes played in concerts at the Mahalia Jackson Theater.

"I got **PEACHES**, **PEARS**, and **APPLES**."

The "P" sound in each word keeps the rhythm like the drums in Congo Square.

"I got
ASPARAGUS."

Mr. Okra's **ASPARAGUS** are thin and tall
like the steeples of the St. Louis Cathedral.

"I got **BROCCOLI**."

His heads of **BROCCOLI** are lush like the
Mediterranean fan palms planted in Jackson Square.

"I got **EGGPLANT**."

The skin of the **EGGPLANT** is as dark as the coffee at Café du Monde.

His **BLUEBERRIES** are the color of the big
BLUE doors at the Louisiana Children's Museum.

"I got **CANTALOUPES**. I got **MANGOES**."

"I got **STRAWBERRIES**. I got **GRAPES**."

All of Mr. Okra's fresh fruits and vegetables are colorful like the magical floats of **MARDI GRAS WORLD**.

"I got **WATERMELON**."

Mr. Okra's **WATERMELONS** are **GREEN** on the outside just like the St. Charles streetcar and **RED** on the inside just like the streetcar on Canal Street.

Mr. Okra's SWEET CORN blooms like flowers in the New Orleans Botanical Gardens.

"I got **SPINACH**. I got **COLLARD GREENS**. I got **MUSTARD GREENS**."

"I got **POTATOES**, **GARLIC**, and **ONIONS**."

"I got **TOMATOES**, **CUCUMBERS**, and **AVOCADOS**."

They are as different as the animals at Audubon Zoo.

BE NICE OR LEAVE!

MR OKRA

At the end of the day, when Mr. Okra is done selling fresh fruits and vegetables, he drives away in his bright **RED** truck carrying his produce like a big cargo ship on the Mississippi River.